Software Engineer

Other titles in the *Cutting Edge Careers* series include:

Software Engineer

Bitsy Kemper

ReferencePoint Press®

San Diego, CA

To Mitchell, an engineer in the making.

© 2018 ReferencePoint Press, Inc.
Printed in the United States

For more information, contact:
ReferencePoint Press, Inc.
PO Box 27779
San Diego, CA 92198
www.ReferencePointPress.com

LIBRARY OF CONGRESS CATALOGING-IN-PUBLICATION DATA

Name: Kemper, Bitsy, author.
Title: Software engineer/by Bitsy Kemper.
Description: San Diego, CA: ReferencePoint Press, Inc., 2017. | Series: Cutting edge careers | Includes bibliographical references and index. | Audience: Grades 9 to 12.
Identifiers: LCCN 2016056796 (print) | LCCN 2017000534 (ebook) | ISBN 9781682821886 (hardback) | ISBN 9781682821893 (eBook)
Subjects: LCSH: Software engineering--Vocational guidance--Juvenile literature. | Computer programmers--Juvenile literature.
Classification: LCC QA76.758 .K465 2017 (print) | LCC QA76.758 (ebook) | DDC 005.1092--dc23
LC record available at https://lccn.loc.gov/2016056796

CONTENTS

SOFTWARE ENGINEER AT A GLANCE

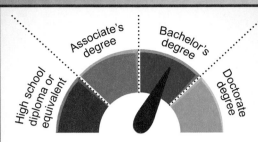

Minimum Educational Requirements

High school diploma or equivalent • Associate's degree • Bachelor's degree • Doctorate degree

Personal Qualities

- ☑ Creative thinking
- ☑ Problem-solving skills
- ☑ Analytical skills
- ☑ Detail oriented
- ☑ Math and technical skills

Working Conditions

Indoors

Median Salary $100,690 per year

1.1 MILLION

Number of jobs as of 2014

Growth Rate

17%

Future Job Outlook

Technology Is Everywhere

Technology has become so prevalent that it touches nearly every aspect of modern life. It aids scientific as well as artistic explorations and has become part and parcel of everyday conveniences like ATM cards, cell phones, stereos, smart watches, washing machines, and ovens. As a result, most people forget that technology is even there or underestimate its impact on everyday living.

Computer technology is integrated into shopping, socializing, medical advances, and even self-driving cars. Watches are connected to laptops, which are connected to heart rate monitors, which might be connected directly to computers in a doctor's office—and all of these devices rely on software. "It is difficult to imagine a device, system, or organization today that performs some meaningful function and does not depend on software in some way,"[1] says Mikko Varpiola, the cofounder of Codenomicon, a company that develops and markets software testing tools. From alarm clocks to coffee machines to traffic lights, a teen could easily encounter twenty forms of computers before even getting to school in the morning.

A computer's most important component is its microprocessor or central processing unit (CPU). Microprocessors are found in just about every electronic device and appliance, not just in laptops or smartphones. Coffee makers, toasters, and refrigerators have microprocessors. So do elevators, automobiles, remote-control toys, pool equipment, airplanes, game controllers, karaoke machines, and identification cards.

All of these electronic devices require software to enable them to communicate with the microprocessor. Medical equipment, military surveillance technology, and machines that facilitate cancer research all depend on electronic interaction and, therefore, software. *Every* electronic device with a CPU needs software.

Software Makes It All Possible

Software is a collection of instructions that enables a user to interact with a computer or electronic device. An electronic device can be anything from a garage door opener to a fitness tracker. Without software, computers and electronic devices would be useless. Software is what tells all of those tiny pieces of metal and silicon how to work with each other. It is like giving the different pieces of hardware a common language to speak. The two pieces, hardware and software, are planned together from the start. Neither can work without the other.

Today virtually all hardware is designed with its software in mind. "By its simplest definition, software is a set of instructions that tell the microprocessor what to do," says software engineer Matt Reisner. "So, it's not that software is an afterthought. Software is a *requirement* of most modern devices. In fact, nearly all modern electronic hardware is designed specifically to run software."[2] ABI Research, a company that provides technological advice to businesses, estimates that as of 2017 more than 10 billion electronic devices were networked together. Software makes all that networking possible—and behind every piece of software is a software engineer.

The People Behind the Program

Software engineers are the people behind computer programs, which include every kind of software and application (app), including those that run Facebook and Snapchat. Some software engineers develop apps that allow people to do specific tasks on a computer or another device, such as send e-mails using a program like Gmail or Outlook or edit photos using a program like Photoshop. Other software engineers develop and create the underlying systems that run the devices or that control networks, like Windows, Mac OS, or networking software.

Software engineers either design an original piece of software or improve an existing one to make it better, faster, or cheaper. Some software engineers come up with ideas for programs that have never existed, or they imagine how a piece of software can be improved and whether and how it can be done. Their job often involves writing a lot of computer code. It also involves fixing (or debugging) a lot of code. Either way, software engineers work with an array of different coding languages to design, plan, and test the software that touches virtually every aspect of modern life.

CHAPTER 1

What Does a Software Engineer Do?

Software engineers design, develop, and test the software used by every kind of electronic device. They also create, test, and evaluate the applications that make computers and electronic devices work. Basically, software engineers translate hardware data into a language each device can understand and then turn that content into something a human can understand. They write a code called logic that controls the interactions between different parts of the hardware itself (such as between the CPU and the motherboard—the heart of the computer where all the main circuits are stored), the hardware and devices/drivers (such as between the motherboard and printers), the hardware and operating system (such as between the motherboard and Windows), and the operating system and software (such as between Windows and Word).

Creating software is also known as designing, writing, or coding. Engineers use different programming languages when they create software, depending on the purpose of the program and the computing environment in which the program runs. Although highly industry dependent, the programming languages most often used are C, C++, Java, Javascript, .NET, and Python. "Last I heard, there are over four hundred software languages," said a senior software engineer who works for a government defense contractor. "Many factors go into deciding which language is ideal for each situation."[3]

Software engineers might be called software designers, developers, or programmers, depending on which specific tasks they perform. However, all are grouped under the heading of software engineer. In general, software engineers are divided into two categories: applications engineers and systems engineers. Typically they work at the same company doing different parts of the same project or work individually on separate tasks.

Apps Engineers

Computer applications software engineers are called apps engineers. They focus on creating programs. An apps engineer typically does not build an entire app alone. He or she works with other apps engineers to construct an app, much the way a house is built using carpenters, welders, plumbers, tilers, and so on. Different engineers with different specialties work on different aspects of the application.

As a whole, apps engineers design, construct, deploy, and maintain general computer applications software, such as Microsoft Outlook, Excel, or PowerPoint. They might also work on specialized programs that are specifically designed for a company or a product, such as the contact information forms used by a school. The most effective apps engineers build software programs by analyzing the needs of end users—the people who will end up using the software or product.

Software engineers spend the bulk of their working hours at their computers. They design, develop, and test software. They also create, test, and evaluate applications for computers and electronic devices.

Some apps engineers work together to develop prepackaged computer applications that are sold to the general public. Examples of such apps include the game Angry Birds or the social platform Snapchat. Apps engineers can create larger customized programs for companies to use for things like inventory or call-center tracking. Some of these engineers also develop custom databases, such as a specific program that the National Football League might want created to keep track of college team names, coaches, scoring percentages, and lineups for an entire division for recruiting purposes. Retired Intel software engineer Mark Russell created a custom program called Dolch Tally that searches for and tallies a specific list of words in text documents. Writers use it to track common word usage and reading level in their manuscripts.

> "Development is the breath of a software engineer—it's what we live for. There's nothing more exciting than creating something new."[4]
>
> —Nicholas C. Zakas, software engineer

For creative types, idea creation and development is often considered the best part of apps engineering. "Development is the breath of a software engineer—it's what we live for. There's nothing more exciting than creating something new,"[4] says software engineer Nicholas C. Zakas, who was a lead developer for Yahoo.

Computer Programmers: A Subset of Apps Engineers

Computer programmers are also software engineers. They are tasked with writing programs. "It used to be 'programmer' but now you hear 'software developer' or 'software architect' for higher-level people or team leads, and yes, many programmers refer to themselves simply as 'software engineer,'" says engineer Matt Reisner. "I see job postings all the time that use these terms interchangeably."[5]

After a program's functionality and purpose are designed and laid out, the programmer converts that design into an ordered series of instructions that the computer executes. These instructions are often broken down into smaller commands, which are broken down further into bits of code. The programmer codes these instructions in any of a number of programming languages, the same ones used by engineers. Computer programmers also update, repair, modify, and expand existing programs. Some large projects involve many programmers who might work on their own piece of a project or work together with other programmers and engineers on a large project.

The line between software engineer and computer programmer is blurring. As software design has become more advanced, some programming functions have become automated. As those tasks become automated, programmers have risen to assume responsibilities that were once performed only by software engineers. As a result, some computer programmers now help software engineers identify user needs and design certain parts of computer programs as well as other functions. "Software engineers (usually the more senior folks) typically design/construct systems whereas programmers then use the designs and guidance to construct specific software," explains Bill Draven, who is a type of software engineer known as an integration architect. "[It is] sort of the same idea as an architect and construction worker working together in the building industry."[6]

Systems Engineers

Most large companies have their own organized computer system. "Someone needs to determine how many servers will be needed, how to configure the network, which includes wi-fi, how to secure the network, and many other computer-related decisions," explains Reisner. "Setup and maintenance of every computer and software application within the company falls within the job description of systems engineer."[7] Systems engineers are in charge of configuring and coordinating this system. In short, they plan, develop, test, and supervise computer hardware and computer networks. They also oversee the system's installation, maintenance, and expansion to make sure it is functioning properly. They make sure the computers are working well and that the servers that work with the laptops and desktops are stable and running.

Seeing Software Engineering

What does trying on sunglasses have to do with software? For Roopa Desa, the senior engineering manager at eyewear service company Eyefinity, it means everything. The programs she and her team of software engineers work on help doctors, patients, and eyeglass vendors. When patients come in for an eye exam, their information, eyeglass prescription specifications, and insurance details are all entered into a software program that Desa and her team created. The same program is used by the lab that makes the lenses to fill the order and by the vision insurance company to collect money and track claims.

Some programs offered by Eyefinity are based on customer feedback. For example, Desa and her team received feedback that customers did not want to spend so much time trying on glasses in a doctor's office. So they created a program that allows them to try on hundreds of different frames virtually. "A patient can click a selfie and virtually try on various frames from home or anywhere," says Desa. They can do it "from their couch, without having to go into the doctor's office. . . . Software made it all possible."

Roopa Desa, interview with author, November 9, 2016.

A systems engineer also might work with the information technology (IT) department to set up the organization's Internet access and ensure each device can properly connect to it. Some companies have thousands of networked devices, from large confidential servers to hundreds of smartphones that require constant and uninterrupted service. Systems engineers also work on intranets—networks that link computers within an organization so employees can more easily communicate with each other.

Systems engineers are also usually responsible for designing and implementing data and application security. In other words, they are in charge of making sure sensitive data cannot be hacked. As such, system engineers write programs that scramble data unless it is accessed correctly, which makes it nearly impossible to steal the information. They created Blu-ray DVDs, for example, which have encoded data that make it harder to illegally copy the content. Systems engineers can also create firewalls and security checks to make sure only authorized people have access. This is very important in the military, for example, where classified information can only be accessed by people who have software-secured identification badges that grant them admission to physically secured areas.

Staying One Step Ahead

Keeping company information safe from hackers is often high on a business owner's priority list. Data breaches, hacking, and cyberattacks are on the rise, making a software engineer's job crucial. Ben Kepes of the technology magazine *Network World* reports, "There is a continuing escalation in both the size and frequency of attacks . . . an average of 124,000 events per week over the last 18 months and a 73 percent increase in peak attack size over 2015."[8] The only way for companies to keep their information safe is to hire software engineers to develop hack-proof programs.

Engineers must implement these programs one step ahead of the hackers. In late 2016, for example, software engineers created a program called Shuffler to constantly scramble code as a program runs, which makes it much more difficult for hackers to execute a cyberattack. "Shuffler makes it nearly impossible to turn a bug into a functioning attack, defending software developers from their mistakes," says the study's lead author, David Williams-King, an engineering graduate student at Columbia University. "Attackers are unable to figure out the program's layout if the code keeps changing."[9]

In 2014 one of the largest-ever IT attacks was reported at a German steel mill. Workers were targeted with booby-trapped e-mails, and once the perpetrators got insider access to the business network, hackers were able to burrow into the control systems network that operated the equipment on the production floor. The hackers' interference caused a furnace to catch fire, resulting in major property damage. Equipment failed and mill workers were unable to quickly understand, contain, or stop the failures. Engineering consultants like Greg A. Lynch contend that if the company had had software engineers on staff to encrypt code and a systems engineer to monitor what was going on, the breach could have been avoided. "This is a preventable crime,"[10] Lynch says.

Another large and well-known security breach involved Target stores. After a hacking incident in 2013, the company said as many as 110 million people may have had personal information, such as e-mail addresses and phone numbers, stolen. At least 40 million credit cards were also compromised, which required Target to reimburse banks $39.4 million for fraudulent charges and other costs associated with replacing cards that people were reluctant to use after the breach. Hiring more software engineers is thus key to overcoming future breaches and maintaining customer peace of mind. "It becomes a reputational risk issue," says Alex Barinka of Bloomberg News. "These kinds of issues used to not be on the tops of the minds [of chief executive officers]. . . . Now they are."[11]

> "A really nice thing about software engineering is that if you have a good idea, you can implement it right away."[12]
>
> —Xiaoyun Yang, software engineer

Defending Against Insiders

Data thieves do not only lurk outside of a company; increasingly, company insiders are the ones who perpetrate data breaches. In fact, a 2016 study found that 74 percent of chief information security officers were concerned about their own employees stealing sensitive company information. As a result, some companies hire systems engineers to solely work in security. Those engineers keep a watchful eye both inside and outside company lines. For instance, if a fast food company has a secret recipe so classified that even the employees cannot access it, they will hire a software engineer to create a sort of virtual safe featuring complex passwords and codes to ensure the recipe is not leaked.

There are many ways an engineer can go about designing cybersecurity solutions or any other piece of software. Many software engineers appreciate the technical as well as creative possibilities the job offers. "A really nice thing about software engineering is that if you have a good idea, you can implement it right away," says engineer Xiaoyun Yang. She points out that the software industry evolves rapidly and requires one to constantly learn new tools and concepts. "Software engineers need to be resourceful and know when to leverage an existing technology . . . and when it's necessary to create something new."[12]

CHAPTER 2

How Do You Become a Software Engineer?

Although a bachelor's degree is often required to become a software engineer, one can start preparing much earlier than that. One way to get a head start on a career in software engineering is to take the right balance of classes in high school.

What to Take in High School

Software engineering requires a solid foundation in mathematics, so exposure to mathematical concepts is critical. Math courses for budding software engineers include algebra, geometry, trigonometry, statistics, and calculus. "Most software engineering . . . comes down to nothing but *mathematics*," says Google software engineer Gaurav Jha. "It doesn't matter how many [programming] languages you know or how cool you are with Java, C, C++, etc."[13]

Computer-related classes are also useful in high school. These include computer science, web design, or any kind of software-related course. "My high school offered three software development classes, and I took all three," says Bradley Stewart of Shareable Ink, a company focused on digitizing health care. "There was a web design course, visual basic course and a C++ course. I would most definitely recommend them where offered."[14]

> "Most software engineering . . . comes down to nothing but *mathematics*."[13]
>
> —Gaurav Jha, Google software engineer

However, software engineers need to have a firm grasp of other subjects too. Michael Bolin, a former Google engineer, stresses the need for a solid foundation in English. "I expect many readers to be surprised that English is second in my list, ranking above science [after math]," he writes on his website. "As a software engineer, I spend a lot of time reading email, writing email,

Students work together on a programming project. School clubs that focus on computers, engineering, and robotics offer a chance to practice new skills and meet people with similar interests.

writing documentation, and communicating via instant messenger. . . . Therefore, being able to write well is an important skill for a software engineer. This includes grammar and spelling!"[15]

Clubs and Independent Projects

Classes are not the only way students can learn the skills and subjects that go toward becoming a software engineer—some high schools offer computing, programming, or robotics clubs that meet during lunch or after school. These are worth exploring—or starting, if your school does not yet have one. For example, students and faculty at Rockhurst High School in Kansas City, Missouri, created a software engineering club. There, students gather to work on software projects, plan activities such as robotics competitions, and perform community service. The club provides technical resources that create opportunities for students to explore software development. "Joining clubs is great and lets

Taking Class or Going Rogue

Some students ready themselves to become software engineers by taking the right mix of classes. Colleges have different requirements, but most feature the same set of core classes. These include computer programming, program design, computer systems analysis, the fundamentals of hardware, networking, computer architecture, professional awareness, mathematics for computing, databases, and academic skills for computing. Statistics, algebra, and calculus are important math classes to take. Other relevant classes include English, graphic design, logic, psychology, and personnel management.

Other software engineers, however, are self-taught and have not taken any college classes. As Katie Bouwkamp from the coding boot camp Coding Dojo puts it, "Computer programming is a trade, and it can be taught in the same manner that someone can learn how to use Adobe Photoshop." Software developer Dave Aronson agrees. "Everything you need, you can learn on your own (mainly online), for free," he says. Yet both Bouwkamp and Aronson acknowledge that college degrees carry more weight, and advancement takes much longer without one. However, pursuing a software engineering career without a formal degree might be an option for some quick learners and motivated self-starters.

Katie Bouwkamp, "How to Become a Software Developer: The Top 6 Myths Holding You Back," *Coding Dojo Blog*, August 15, 2015. www.codingdojo.com.

Quoted in Quora, "What College Classes Do I Need to Take to Be a Software Engineer?," Software Engineering Career Advice, October 23, 2015. www.quora.com.

you talk to like-minded individuals," says Iliya Koreshev, a senior software engineer at the large gaming company Zynga.

However, Koreshev also stresses the importance of pursuing projects on one's own. "Sometimes it just happens that there are not that many people in computer clubs," says Koreshev. "If you really like computers and figuring out how they work both at a basic level of the circuits and at a higher level of the software running on them, then your best bet is to start doing some projects on your own time."[16] It may turn out that spending time coding at home is the best use of one's free time. Students can also advance their knowledge by taking advantage of in-depth online resources like Khan Academy or EngineerGirl; local after-school classes; or specialized, intensive summer camps, such as Google's three-week Computer Science Summer Institute or the seven-week Girls Who Code Summer Immersion Program. The Engineering Education Service Center offers a list of summer camps broken down by state.

College and Beyond

Software engineers are expected to hold a bachelor's degree in computer science, software engineering, or mathematics. Systems engineers often study computer science or computer information systems. Apps engineers often study the same subjects, but they are also likely to take graphic design and psychology to understand how to make effective and user-friendly interfaces. "You can stand out from the typical engineering student by taking extra courses in psychology,"[17] encourages Barbara Oakley, an engineering professor at Oakland University in Michigan.

Software engineers who work on scientific or engineering applications usually need a degree in computer or information science, mathematics, engineering, or the physical sciences. Those who work on business applications usually need to take college courses in management information systems and business, and they need to possess strong programming skills. Accounting, finance, and production operations management classes are also helpful. Software engineers can also take classes that focus on logical analysis and thinking.

It is not necessary to get a degree in software engineering to become a software engineer. Sometimes software engineers fall into the field after receiving degrees in other areas, such as chemistry, graphic design, or psychology. With hundreds of programming languages used throughout the industry, knowing or being willing to learn new languages can be even more important than the specific college degree that one holds. "In the defense industry, we have technical degrees in physics, aerospace engineering,

A Time to Learn

One of the most important things young software developers can do is participate in an internship. Internships involve working for a company for either relatively low or no pay, usually for ten to twelve weeks. The point of an internship is to gain skills and experience and to learn as much as one possibly can.

Therefore, interns should not be afraid to ask questions and seek out information. According to Shubhro Saha, a software engineer at Facebook, "You might be afraid your work is not up to par, that your code is non-idiomatic, or that people find your questions annoying. Don't worry about it! Yes, people are busy, but effective team members will help you because they care about the overall success of the team." Companies offer internships to build strong programmers to hire in the future, so it is in employees' interests to help interns learn as much as they can.

Shubhro Saha, "Tips for Software Engineering Internships," October 15, 2014. www.shubhro.com.

and the like," says a software engineer who has worked on missiles and satellites. "Interestingly, hardly any of us have computer software degrees. Every job I've had has been in a language I hadn't used yet, so the degree itself didn't seem to matter. We learned on the job."[18]

A four-year college degree is standard for most software engineering positions, although a two-year degree or certificate may be adequate for some computer programming positions. "For some fields, certifications may help, but for others, they won't matter at all,"[19] says Chaka Allen, an independent software consultant at Calcalitics, Inc., a technology consulting company. Many companies will only hire or interview those who have a four-year degree. "An associate's degree is becoming less and less accepted," says software engineer Bill Draven. "Generally, we do not interview anyone without at least a four-year degree."[20]

Graduate degrees come in handy for software engineers who work on complex tasks that require advanced problem-solving and technical skills, as well as for those looking to move up to management positions. A software engineer with a master's degree is prepared to work in just about any industry, from finance to aerospace, and can choose to work at any stage of the software process. If you are already working in the software field, a master's degree won't necessarily net you a different job title, but it could help you vie for more sought-after positions with larger or more popular companies.

Internships Are Valuable

In addition to education, employers highly value relevant experience. Students who want to work in software engineering or programming can increase their odds of finding a job by interning. Large computer and consulting firms often train new employees via intensive company-based internship programs. Private companies, colleges, universities, and government-run labs also offer internships. Some internships are paid, but others are not.

Retired engineer Mark Russell mentored several interns during his time at Intel. He feels such programs help the intern as well as the company. "I worked with quite a few interns and it is rewarding for both parties," he says. "It gives the software intern real-world experience working on actual hardware." In addition to experience, such programs often help interns land a permanent position. "The time spent in the internship can be thought of as a very long interview that can last up to 6 months or more," says Russell. "We have a very good idea on whether to make the intern permanent once they finish school."[21]

> "The time spent in the internship can be thought of as a very long interview that can last up to 6 months or more. We have a very good idea on whether to make the intern permanent once they finish school."[21]
>
> —Mark Russell, retired Intel software engineer

Interns, too, get to see whether the company is a good fit for them. "It wasn't until after I returned to school and my friends and I compared notes about our internships that I realized how good I had it," says engineer Peter Torelli, who interned in two different departments at Intel. He adds:

Some companies didn't let interns use the labs, some friends were stuck writing papers instead of working with circuits, and some groups consisted of much older people, so making friends was hard. Without an internship, I never would have even known to consider those details. Even if I hated my internship, having that experience prepared me to ask critical questions when the time came to find a full-time job.[22]

Continuing Education

A software engineer's education and training does not stop once he or she lands a job. The technology industry is arguably the most rapidly changing industry there is, and people who work in it need to keep pace with changes. This involves taking continuing education and professional development classes offered by employers, colleges, private training institutions, and professional computing societies. "This is not a 'may,' this is a 'must,'" says Draven. "In my experience, technology has a revolution every five years. To keep up, an engineer has to reinvent, retool, and retrain on the same schedule."[23]

Most large companies understand this and thus take continuing education very seriously. Some even pay for it entirely. "When I worked at Intel, they had a generous policy of offering employees continuing education," says Russell. "In my case, I started out with a degree in electronics but found I liked software much more. Intel paid for me to take programming courses. Eventually I went back to school and I got a second degree in software architecture. Intel paid the full bill of $31,000, and I put that degree to full use for them!"[24]

Continuing education does not have to take place at a school. Software engineers can also keep their skills up-to-date by attending conferences and by taking online classes. Likewise, they can stay in tune with advances in the industry via online forums, by reading journal articles and white papers, and by staying active in professional industry organizations like the Institute of Electrical and Electronics Engineers (IEEE).

CHAPTER 3

What Skills and Personal Qualities Matter Most—and Why?

It is no secret that math plays a large role in software engineering. Being proficient in math is key to undertaking any sort of engineering role. As Google software engineer Gaurav Jha puts it, "A full-time software engineering [role] not only requires an ability to work on complex algorithms but enough tolerance and patience to focus on meticulous details of a large program."[25] Excellent problem-solving and analytical skills are also important qualities to possess if one is to become a successful software engineer.

Identifying Problems

Famous baseball manager Yogi Berra once said, "If you don't know where you are going, you'll end up someplace else."[26] Nothing could be more true about software engineering. Before they ever begin design work, software engineers must be able to identify which problems (or needs) their software will aim to solve (or serve). "I consider problem solving the most interesting part of my job. The more complex the better," says software engineer Claudia Galvan, who is president of the Society of Women Engineers, Santa Clara Valley in California. "I like the ability to exercise my analytical and technical skills to innovate and solve big problems."[27] A software engineer must know how to analyze an end user's needs.

> "I consider problem solving the most interesting part of my job. The more complex the better."[27]
>
> —Claudia Galvan, president of the Society of Women Engineers, Santa Clara Valley

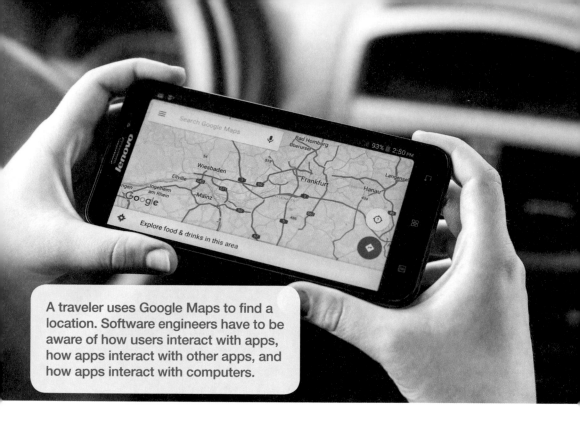

A traveler uses Google Maps to find a location. Software engineers have to be aware of how users interact with apps, how apps interact with other apps, and how apps interact with computers.

Understanding who will need the software, and why, is key to the job. "This is probably the most important thing you do as a software engineer," says engineer Mark Russell. "It's vital to understand what the user is asking for, and to not develop software you *think* they want."[28]

Software engineers need to be able to think about problems in three main ways. First, they must understand problems at their largest level—to see the big picture and be able to break it down into smaller problems. "A good developer can factor large, complex problems into a series of common patterns," explains software engineer Bill Draven. "Identifying common patterns, and solving for them, leads to lower cost and speedier time to market."[29] Software engineers also need to be able to anticipate what potential problems might arise over the long term. They should be able to envision what the problem might look like in one, five, or ten years down the road to ensure the solution will last. At the same time, they need to be able to think small. They must understand a project's finer details in order to plan and implement the short-term steps to complete it.

Computing Skills

A strong foundation in computer science will make the difference between a successful software engineer and an unemployed one. That includes having expertise with databases, networking, algorithms, and programming skills. Russell says knowing about compilers (programs that turn code into a language that the computer's processor can understand) is useful, but he does not think it is an imperative skill. Rather, he suggests software engineers learn about software architecture, which involves understanding the structure of the computer system that is being worked on. "While software architecture tends to be one of the more overlooked skills, I would say it is probably one of the most useful skills," he says. "It allows you to develop the foundation for your project before any code is written. It helps you to catch any potential errors very early in the design, where the cost is much less then it would be after the software construction phase is complete."[30]

Successful software engineers also need to be able to write in multiple code languages. For example, they should be able to write a program in C++ for one project, then be able to switch to Java for a different project. "Just like a person who can speak several languages, an engineer who isn't tied to one code language can think outside the box and is a more desirable hire," note engineers on the *Masters in Software Engineering* blog. "A willingness to learn new languages, new libraries and new ways of building systems goes a long way to creating a great software engineer."[31]

Creative Thinking

Some might be surprised to learn that software engineers must be able to think creatively. Creativity is the process of breaking out of established patterns, which is required when one is engineering new programs. Software engineers must approach existing information in new ways; this is how they solve problems, including ones that have not even been identified yet. For example, the autocorrect feature of every social media and word processing app was a feature added not because anyone asked for it but because a member of the Microsoft Word team was looking at ways to make typing more efficient.

Peer Review? No Pressure

When programmers are typing nearly one hundred words per minute, it is easy for them to make simple typos and syntax errors. For this reason, most code goes through a process of peer review, in which one's work gets reviewed by other software engineers. Kevin Burke, an employee at the logistics company Shyp, states that submitting code for peer review finds 68 to 99 percent of the bugs in the software.

Peer reviews can include things known as regression tests, informal code reviews, new function (component) tests, integration tests, and more. Burke says, "Code reading detected 80 percent more faults per hour than testing." This means that in a lot of cases, having a human go over code can be much more efficient than running digital diagnostic tests. The downfall of having other programmers review code, however, is that the process is substantially more expensive than having a computer do it. However, for smaller projects, such as building a mobile app, having peers edit code is an efficient way to help ensure the program is functioning properly.

Quoted in Kevin Burke, "Why Code Review Beats Testing: Evidence from Decades of Programming Research," October 3, 2011. http://kev.inburke.com.

"What does creativity have to do with software development?" asks software developer Michael Lant. "Actually a lot." Lant points to the Wright brothers, who invented the first airplane, to show how technical knowledge is useless without a strong dose of creativity and a willingness to experiment. "The principles of flight were well known long before the Wright brothers first took to the air," he says. "What they did was find the right combination of bicycle parts, weight, wing surface, engine power, wood and canvas and the right balance point to make the first flight possible."[32]

Attention to Detail

There is no room for error when designing software. One tiny mistake can destroy an entire program and prevent it from running properly. Therefore, engineers must have a keen eye for detail, including finding typos or syntax errors in thousands of lines of code. Large errors—those that result in a program not running at all—are fairly easy to find. The more difficult errors are small ones in which the program functions but is doing the wrong thing. For example, in the popular game Minecraft, when the designer was creating a pig he mistakenly inverted the x- and y-axis in the code. The pig appeared, but it looked wrong. (The designer ended up keeping it and using it as the now-famous monster he calls a creeper.) As software engineer Jha puts it, one needs "meticulous skills to read codes written by others and spot issues in [them]."[33]

Interface design is one example of an area in which attention to detail is crucial. In addition to the program itself, software engineers need to design several interfaces—that is, the process by which any two devices (or combination of people and devices) communicate. Programmers need to pay attention to how a user interacts with an app, how the app interacts with other apps, and how the app interacts with the computer. For example, a browser is an interface between a person and the Internet. A remote is an interface between an end user and a device such as a television, a speaker, or a toy. Some projects might have a human factors engineer whose entire job is to design the detail of the interfaces with which people interact. If a program's interface is not carefully designed or user-friendly, people will be less likely to use the application. Interface designers therefore need to make sure that every detail works just right.

> "[Software engineers need] meticulous skills to read codes written by others and spot issues in [them]."[33]
>
> —Gaurav Jha, Google software engineer

Communication Skills

Software engineers often work in teams comprising other engineers, management, and possibly people from finance, marketing, or other departments. As such, good communication skills are high on the list of qualities software engineers must possess. They must be able to understand what is expected of them, know how to ask clear and specific questions, and be able to work well

Name That Code

Software developers need to excel at labeling things. A single program may use hundreds to thousands of different variables, and being able to name each of them uniquely, distinctly, and recognizably is crucial to creating code that other developers can understand. If there are groups of equations that turn Fahrenheit values to Celsius ones, for example, it would be better to name it *FarToCels* than, say, *Equation.* It is much like clearly naming file folders so you know what is inside. "When you read code that you or someone else has written, you are gaining most of your understanding about that code from the names of things in that code," explains John Sonmez, the founder of the Simple Programmer website, podcast, and YouTube channel, as well as the author of *Soft Skills: The Software Developer's Life Manual.* "It doesn't matter if you can understand something, if you can't adequately explain it, the moment it leaves your head it is gone." Naming each variable coherently, as well as leaving clear developer notes in the code, shows that the developer understands the key principles of software engineering. It also helps any engineers that might come in to change or debug the program in the future.

Quoted in John Sonmez, "The 4 Most Important Skills for a Software Developer," Simple Programmer, December 9, 2012. https://simpleprogrammer.com.

in a group. Doing so is much easier if one has good verbal, listening, and writing skills.

Software engineers also usually need to present ideas—or the end product itself—to nonengineers who will be using, selling, or otherwise interacting with the technology. The ability to explain complex technology in nontechnical terms is very helpful in such situations. This is often done using analogies and common language (instead of so-called geek speak). "If I was explaining data storage to a client and the choices were remote/local/in memory, I could give them simple definitions," says Draven. "I could use a grocery analogy: remote is like groceries at the market, local is like groceries in your cabinet, and in memory is like food cooking on your stove."[34] If an engineer cannot clearly explain his or her product to the customer or nontechnical members of the team, then he or she may as well not have created it in the first place.

A Mix of Skills and Qualities

Matt Weisfeld, a software developer and author, conducted a survey for the online IT learning resource InformIT that asked companies what they look for when hiring programmers. Across the board, companies answered that they want more than smarts. One company explained that its ideal candidate has "the ability to solve problems. The ability to learn new technologies rapidly. The ability to find solutions to problems using the Internet. A mindset of efficiency and creativity."[35] As a representative from one company cited in the survey put it, "Most skills can be learned and improved—what are often times hard to change are a person's nature and character."[36]

This mix of skills needs to be on display before an engineer ever has a job. In fact, he or she should master and be able to demonstrate most of them when interviewing for positions. "The most difficult part about getting hired in the software engineering field is passing the interviews," says software consultant Chaka Allen. "Interviews are, quite often, quizzes on your technical knowledge."[37] Interviews also assess whether an engineer is a good fit for the company. Many hiring companies are looking for candidates with flexibility and a willingness to learn. Dan Yarwood, a programmer at the online ad programming company Adzerk, admits that he "was surprised to find . . . software engineers who interviewed me were, for the most part, not concerned that I had little to no experience with the databases, languages, or frameworks that they use. They were more interested in whether or not I was the kind of person who would be interested and driven enough to learn to use them."[38]

CHAPTER 4

What Is It Like to Work as a Software Engineer?

Software engineers work in just about every industry. Many work for firms that deal in computer systems design, for hardware and software publishers such as Hewlett Packard or Apple, or for companies that rely heavily on software platforms such as Amazon or Facebook. They might work for electronics manufacturing companies such as Intel, Micron, AMD, Samsung, or Motorola. Apps engineers work everywhere, from large corporate office environments in banking, insurance, or security to small one-person businesses. "Most large organizations have so many software apps, an engineer can work for one of many groups within a particular company,"[39] says software engineer Chaka Allen.

Working for either type of company has advantages and disadvantages. Larger companies tend to offer higher pay, job security, benefits such as retirement and low- or no-cost health insurance, and the chance to work for big names like Google or Microsoft. However, an engineer might not have much say when it comes to a program's design or launch details. Since many engineers tend to work on large projects together, each person works on a small piece of the final product. In addition, with so many peers competing for promotions, it can take longer to become a manager or a lead engineer. In a smaller company, software engineers may find they have the flexibility to be more creative and take charge of projects right from the start. Because they have fewer employees, smaller companies can offer a faster path to management, tend to have a more relaxed work environment, and may be able to offer flexible work arrangements. On the flip side, smaller software companies have more riding on each software program, so if one product fails, the entire company may go under.

A Typical Day

A software engineer's typical workday takes place at a desk, in an office, and is usually spent working on several different projects, or pieces of projects, at once. Engineers start their day by checking e-mail, reviewing their calendars, and maybe doing a write-up on a completed project or filing a progress report on a current one. They usually attend a few meetings to update coworkers on the status of current projects or to be briefed on ongoing or new projects.

Meetings may also be called to figure out why a software project is not working and how to fix it—a process called debugging. Many software engineers say that most of their day is spent debugging. Generally speaking, regardless of the industry or task, much of a software engineer's time is spent in meetings analyzing needs (preparing) and then on the computer designing the solutions (doing). When not in meetings or writing reports, a software engineer can get down to business.

Software development requires collaboration. Whether working on design, development, or programming, software engineers typically work as part of a team.

The Collaborative Process

Software development tends to be a collaborative process, which means that engineers usually work on teams to design, develop, and program successful software. Typically, the software process starts with submitting a proposal. A team takes into account the client's desire, from hardware to software to testing to the end product, and includes how much the product will cost to build.

In other cases, a customer might come to the company with an idea for a product he or she wants designed or built. Customers might have unrealistic expectations about what to expect, and it is the software engineering team's job to do its best to meet the expectations yet also explain what is possible or likely to result. "Would YouTube be a success if videos took 9 hours to download? Would Facebook be popular if every page took 15 minutes to load?" asks National Instruments software engineer Owen Pellegrin. "Now you have a concept of the kinds of constraints software engineers have to respect. It's not enough to just solve a problem, I have to make sure that the solution satisfies whatever constraints the customer wants."[40]

After the customer and management approve the project, final details are agreed upon and the work begins. "There are decisions to be made for most projects like which language and what testing platform to use," says one software engineer who works for a defense contractor. Like any project, there are often snags along the way. The same engineer goes on to say, "When something is wrong, the software engineer has to determine if it is a software issue, a hardware issue, or something that is going wrong between the two."[41] This debugging effort may require the help of more team members. It may also require meetings between hardware engineers, mechanical or electrical engineers, designers, and others.

As an example, when the software engineer and her team discovered that a wheel on a satellite was put together incorrectly,

> "It's not enough to just solve a problem, I have to make sure that the solution satisfies whatever constraints the customer wants."[40]
>
> —Owen Pellegrin, software engineer at National Instruments

A Day in the Life of a Riot Games Software Engineer

A software engineer named Teng describes what it is like to work for the video game and e-sports tournament organizer Riot Games:

[8:00 a.m.:] We give each other visibility on where we are on project fronts, and discuss the opportunities for collaboration. . . .

I'll comb through the backlog and bug list briefly. . . . If there are code reviews or easy fixes, I'll nail them down before meeting up with the team.

[10:00 a.m.:] Standup [meeting]; a quick huddle with the other engineers where we find out what everybody is up to and help out where needed. I give a brief summary of my project progress and map out my plan for the day before tossing out an architectural question.

The next two hours I'll spend crushing some meaty portions of the coding work I'm currently doing. . . .

[After lunch:] Play some *League*. . . .

[2:00 p.m.:] It's time to dive deep into the code ocean again. Two more hours fly, and I've got a bi-weekly dev [development] retro [team meeting]. It's a chance to reflect on ourselves, identify areas where we rock and where our chords are clumsy. We also generate action items. . . .

[5:00 p.m.:] I'm ready to spend a half-hour or two playing around with interesting tech or game dev.

Riot Games, "Day in the Life: Software Engineer," July 7, 2016. www.riotgames.com.

they discussed a variety of ways to solve the problem. Ultimately, they decided to do it with software. "It was much more cost effective to make the change with software than to bring the satellite down and fix the wheel itself,"[42] she says. The work was a collaborative effort from start to finish, and the software engineer was involved in every step.

Work Atmosphere

Like most office workers, software engineers work at their desks, in cubicles or offices, and attend daily team meetings in conference rooms. Companies like Google, SAS, and smaller start-ups are known for their relaxed atmospheres that feature flexible hours, a casual dress code of jeans or shorts, free snacks, and open relaxation rooms where employees can play Ping-Pong or sit on bean bag chairs. Other companies like Intel and Micron are more traditionally corporate; their software departments still work in cubicles, enforce a standard 8 a.m. to 5 p.m. workday, and maintain a more businesslike dress code.

Regardless of corporate culture or industry, software engineers spend much of their day working on a computer. Many describe long hours spent typing on a keyboard—designing, coding, debugging—as repetitive and monotonous. Sometimes it can even be a bit boring. "Software engineering is not as fun as the popular notion says about it," says Google software engineer Gaurav Jha. "Your screen will be Black, Boring & Dull."[43]

The work environment is also overwhelmingly male. Software engineers tend to be predominantly men, and many in the field have said the industry is not very welcoming to women. In fact, female software engineers reportedly earn $10,000 less than their male counterparts. "Three-quarters of women are noticing that they are less well-compensated, and that could be a factor for why they are dropping out"[44] of the tech industry, says Michele Madansky, one of the authors of the Elephant in the Valley survey, which looked at issues women face in the tech workplace. The long hours many software engineers must put in may be an obstacle for working mothers, further adding to the low number of female engineers. "I think if the vast majority of high tech software and engineering companies in the private sector want to get more women into the field—which many say

> "If the vast majority of high tech software and engineering companies in the private sector want to get more women into the field . . . they are ultimately going to need a more flexible work culture."[45]
>
> —Jennifer Sirp, software engineer

they do—they are ultimately going to need a more flexible work culture," says software engineer Jennifer Sirp. "After my son was born, I couldn't find anything that was three to four days a week, even if I was looking into stuff below my pay grade and degree like technical writing, tech support, etc."[45]

Earnings

Male or female, it is true that many software engineers work more than the standard forty hours a week. According to the US Bureau of Labor Statistics (BLS), most software engineers work full time, and long hours are common. It is typical for engineers to work evenings and weekends to meet deadlines, monitor experiments, and/or test new software. There may be times when engineers work from home; it depends on company policy and project needs. "Sometimes you end up staying up all night working on a project just to finish it on time, sometimes you work the entire weekend, sometimes you have to cancel all your plans because you have to work," says software engineer Iliya Koreshev. "I have had to pull multiple all-nighters while working in a startup environment since there are less engineers, less time, and more expectation. When I started working in more established companies this pretty much stopped."[46]

The good news is that engineers are well paid for the long hours they spend on the job. According to the BLS, the median wage for software engineers in 2015 was $100,690, far above the national average ($36,200 for all occupations). Computer occupations overall had a median income of $81,430. The lowest-paid 10 percent of software engineers earned less than $57,340, and the highest-paid 10 percent earned more than $153,710. Typically, engineers are salaried, meaning they are paid an annual wage instead of being paid per hour. However, software engineers who work as consultants or contractors—on a per-project basis rather than as an employee of a company—often charge by the hour. "Independent consultants can earn $100 per hour or more to help companies implement projects," says Allen. "Since they can also manage more than one project at a time, for brief periods of time, the opportunity for growth and income is wide open."[47]

Paychecks are different for contractors. Contractors tend to work hourly and bill their clients accordingly. "I'd say you don't typically see recent college graduates as contractors. Generally speaking, consultants are leading-edge specialists in a given software or type of architecture. It takes years to get to that level of experience,"[48] says software engineer Bill Draven.

CHAPTER 5

Advancement and Other Job Opportunities

Paths to success vary in every field and industry and from person to person. One software engineer's goal may be to get promoted to higher technical titles within an organization. Another engineer may want to be promoted to a management position. Another engineer may want to specialize in a particular area and become a consultant in that field.

Many organizations have official technical tracks and management tracks that match these different goals. "[Engineers] can continue along the technical path and grow into principal engineers and fellows and be senior technical experts in their given area," comments Andy Vargas, the senior principal engineer for Intel. Or, he says, "they can also pursue other paths such as program or project management and people management, which can lead to roles as directors, general managers and vice president."[49] Programmer Andriy Buday simplifies software engineering career advancement this way: "The more you interact with people the more you become [a] leader of [a] team. . . . The less you interact with people the more you become an expert. . . . The more you interact with a company the more you become CEO."[50]

Regardless of which track an engineer chooses, each lays out a path of advancement and an estimate of how many years of experience are required for each step along the path. For example, an engineer might take communication and management classes to prepare for a career in corporate management.

> "The more you interact with people the more you become [a] leader of [a] team. . . . The less you interact with people the more you become an expert."[50]
>
> —Andriy Buday, programmer

39

Classes in advanced technical skills would prepare the employee who prefers the technical route.

Starting Out

As with any industry, most software engineers start their career by taking an entry-level computer software job and working their way up from there. The entry-level engineer is given tasks such as making minor software edits and conducting basic tests to make sure the code is working right. A new hire might also start out on the test design engineering team. Test design engineers define how to test the product or software program and then perform the hands-on testing. A test engineer is also the one who runs tests to verify that code is operational.

Once that skill set has been mastered, the engineer can become a designer. A designer, or architect, is someone who understands the impact of design decisions and can grasp the full extent of what the product will need to do. Designers create a sort of blueprint, which might be a simple flow chart or diagrams to illustrate the architecture of the software, and pass it on to the programmers and collaborative team developing the program. The designer title is gained only after proper experience. Ease of use and performance are some of the things designers implement in their software.

Specialization

In the same way that many basketball players want to keep playing basketball and not move on to coaching, many engineers want to remain engineers. It is therefore possible to succeed as a software engineer without rising through a corporation's ranks. If one sticks to a technical path, job titles might not change much. The career path instead becomes one of specialization, meaning that the engineer's knowledge grows in a particular area (in breadth or depth). Companies appreciate good, smart engineers and want them to stay technical. As software consultant Chaka Allen notes, "One can advance in pay without ever advancing in management. Software developers are rare, and experience can garner significant wages."[51]

A software engineer who gets very good at one aspect of the job might want to focus only on that area. Some specialized engineers even decide to open a consulting company dedicated to that particular specialty, which might be networking, data security concerns, computer information systems, tech support, computer management systems, or web development.

In *The Passionate Programmer*, author Chad Fowler discusses how to find and fill specialized needs, such as being the person who knows how to make outdated technology work with the latest revision. He says an engineer with a specialized skill set is bound to be marketable, get hired, and even earn more money. He emphasizes the importance of letting others know your specialized expertise: "Have a mission. Make sure people know it."[52]

> "One can advance in pay without ever advancing in management. Software developers are rare, and experience can garner significant wages."[51]
>
> —Chaka Allen, independent software consultant

Management

If management rather than specialization is the engineer's goal, he or she will strive to become a project manager. In this role, the engineer is tasked with not only making sure that projects are completed on time and on budget but also with ensuring that all of the engineers involved—from entry-level engineers to test engineers and on up—are doing their jobs. The project manager is often the interface between the customer and those doing the work, as they will tell the team of programmers what the customer wants in the program. Project managers also report progress to upper management.

Project managers do not need to fully understand the technology in order to successfully manage a project, as they are not the ones who actually design or program it. However, a manager does need to be able to effectively communicate key information about the project. Good managers also are skilled at understanding the people who work under them, especially their capabilities and limitations.

Titles and Roman Numerals

As software engineers gain experience, education, and skill, they can move up in position. A software engineer's job level is often indicated by a Roman numeral that follows his or her job title. The higher the number, the more senior the position:

I: Junior engineer
II: Engineer
III: Senior engineer
IV: Principal engineer
V: Fellow or advisory engineer
VI: Consulting engineer

On a programmer's website called Stack Exchange, engineer Erik Engbrecht further explains what the numbers mean. "New hires are generally I or II depending on education. People generally hit III relatively quickly, and tend to stay in there for a while. The majority [of] people never make it past IV," he says. "V is used as an alternative to a manager title while the person is assuming a management-like role. . . . V requires publications and recommendations from both senior management and senior technical staff. VI [traditionally] requires national or international recognition."

Quoted in Stack Exchange, "Software Engineering," January 20, 2011. http://softwareengineering.stackex change.com.

A project manager can be promoted to program manager, a position in which he or she oversees an entire program that consists of many projects. For example, consider a website that lets people buy and sell used cars. One project manager might be in charge of getting all of the servers running and stable; meanwhile, another project manager would be in charge of designing the user interface. The program manager is in charge of the whole thing, making sure all of the different projects fit together. Program managers often have financial responsibilities, such as creating and/ or managing the program budget. Some companies consider the title "program manager" to be on par with "vice president."

Program managers can be promoted to the position of systems designer. Systems designers are not considered management and do not deal with budget concerns. Rather, they are in charge of designing entire systems as opposed to single programs. For example, Windows is an operating system that runs software programs. A systems designer would design Windows, not the software programs Windows runs (such as Word or Excel).

The highest level a software engineer can achieve is that of chief information officer (CIO) or chief technical officer (CTO). These positions have large-scale budgetary responsibilities and usually preside over programs with budgets in the millions or billions of dollars. CIOs and CTOs are also responsible for a large number of employees and contractors in the organization— hundreds to thousands of employees in some cases. Both roles involve organizing overall company strategy, from hiring and firing to maintaining budgets and setting management structure.

Noncorporate Paths to Success

Other software engineers forgo the corporate route in favor of teaching. These engineers work in schools, colleges, and universities, where they use their technical knowledge, experience, and expertise to teach students about software engineering. Much like the corporate world, there are many paths and opportunities to succeed in academia. To teach at the college level, a software engineer would likely start out as a teaching assistant and work up to tenured professor.

Software engineering recruitment can also be a career choice for people who enjoy technology but prefer to work on the people and placement side of things. Recruiters seek out the perfect candidates to fill open positions at hiring companies. In the technology industry, the recruitment field is worth considering because software engineers are in high demand. Many companies look for outside help in hiring qualified people to fill vacant spots. Recruiters who have a background in software engineering are well positioned to understand a job's technical requirements, so they may be uniquely qualified to find candidates who have the right skill set for the job opening.

CHAPTER 6

What Does the Future Hold for Software Engineers?

The future looks bright for software engineers. The BLS projects an employment growth rate of 17 percent through 2024. This is more than twice as fast as the average for all occupations (7 percent), and slightly higher than overall computer occupations, which are expected to grow 12 percent during the same period. Looking at raw data, the actual number of jobs is expected to grow from 1,114,000 to 1,300,600, an increase of 186,600 new positions.

Those software engineers will help create a future unlike anything experienced before. Mathematician Alan J. Perlis has described the relationship between humans and computers as having "a vitality like a gangly youth growing out of his clothes within an endless puberty."[53] It seems the moment a new technology comes out and is enjoyed by the masses, another even newer technology is ready to be launched the next day. Neither users nor creators seem to want to lessen the pace. Translation: Technology is skyrocketing. It is everywhere and it is not slowing down.

Software engineers are poised on the cutting edge of this modernization. As the authors of a 2016 IEEE article put it, "Software already prevents car collisions, helps fight human trafficking and predict genocide, enables electronic prescriptions and health records that save thousands of lives, and has changed how doctors perform lifesaving surgeries."[54] Software engineers are the brains and hands behind those cutting-edge technologies; they are the ones who take them from idea to reality.

In the coming years, software engineers will likely play a part in solving all sorts of problems ranging from identity theft to vehicle malfunctions to emergency response delays to flaws in airport and air traffic control systems.

On the Cutting Edge of Health Care

In health care, for example, software engineers play an important role in developing the latest medical technology. In the biomedical field, software engineers work in hospitals creating programs to track critical medical history as well as in research labs alongside chemists who file and examine clinical studies. They also work on the manufacturing side, fine-tuning state-of-the-art test equipment and working on biomedical devices such as robotic arms used in surgery.

Some of these software engineers design and implement complex imaging systems, such as next-generation computed tomography and magnetic resonance imaging devices. They also write artificial intelligence algorithms to aid in diagnostics and decision making regarding patient care, such as sending health care data collected by a smart watch directly to a computer system at a doctor's office. Software engineers also work on data analysis and modeling software for gene mapping and public health research, helping find cures for diseases. According to the BLS, engineering employment in biomedicine alone is expected to grow 27 percent by the year 2022. Software engineers will account for a large part of that growth.

Advances in Miniaturization

The miniaturization of technology is also bringing about new products and ideas. The IEEE reports the possibility of scientists and engineers creating "millions of cooperating robot modules, each perhaps no bigger than a grain of sand, together mimicking the look and feel of just about anything." They hope that one day these smart particles—dubbed claytronics—will be able to produce real, tangible goods that people can touch and experience without virtual reality goggles or gloves. The applications of this work are almost endless. Someday people might be able to take a lump of claytronic goop and transform it into a coffee cup, a screwdriver, or a toy car, just by moving it around like sand. The challenges in making cool technology like this a reality is not in hardware; it lies in software. *IEEE Spectrum* reports, "The key challenge is not in manufacturing the circuits but in programming the massively distributed system that will result from putting all the units together."[55]

Data-Driven Engineering

Data-driven engineering is another cutting-edge field for software engineers. Data-driven engineering involves using what is known—or can be learned—about users' habits, preferences, and dislikes to build software that is personally tailored to their preferences.

In today's world, users can easily submit feedback about software products in app stores, social media, or user groups. Software designers are eager to collect this feedback in order to better understand, and therefore better serve, their customers. Especially in the gaming world, software engineers use players' thoughts—and complaints—about product features and failings to build better games from the start.

Using tracking placed in the software, engineers can access usage data and error logs from hundreds of thousands of players, including what time they logged on, how long they played, which level they stayed on the longest, and more. They can then use that information to revise future games or build new ones. By watching how a product is being used and incorporating the feedback submitted by real customers, software engineers can look at the habits of users around the globe to help them decide what to develop. "Tomorrow's applications will . . . leverage calendar data, location data, historic clickstream data, social contacts, information from wearables, and much more," says engineer Dries Buytaert. "All that rich data will be used as the input for predictive analytics and personalization services. Eventually, data-driven experiences will be the norm."[56]

> "Tomorrow's applications will . . . leverage calendar data, location data, historic clickstream data, social contacts, information from wearables, and much more."[56]
>
> —Software engineer Dries Buytaert

The Internet of Things

Software engineers also have a critical role to play in the digital future known as the Internet of Things (IoT). The IoT describes the coordination and automation of everyday items. It includes electronic devices like smartphones or fitness bands but also vehicles (from military planes to golf carts); appliances (from washing machines to DNA analyzers); specialized research equipment (such as a human-made electronic clam placed in the middle of the ocean by a marine biologist); entire buildings, wired for connectivity (from solar panels to temperature sensors to employee badge entry systems); and any other item that is embedded with electronics, software, or sensors and is connected to a network that enables it to collect and exchange data.

The IoT will continue to drive the need for technology and thus the need for software engineers. Objects that lack computing capability today will likely have it in the future. Soon all refrigerators will know their contents and will let their owners know when they

Self-Driving Cars Are the Future

In the near future, self-driving cars might be the norm—and software engineering will be responsible for this feat. To allow cars to operate completely by themselves, software engineers have to write thousands of complex commands to ensure the car does not malfunction. This includes outfitting it with special sensors to keep it within its lane, giving it an automatic braking system, and letting it maintain cruise control. All of these features require very precise and advanced software. "The Saturn V rockets that took men to the moon were wind-up toys compared to the 100 million lines of code embedded in a modern Mercedes-Benz," says Jeff Zurschmeide, an author of eight automotive books. "That fact puts software companies front and center when it comes to developing your next car."

Experimental cars are already being tested around the world. Although experimental models have been reported as clumsy, many people are eager to get the driverless cars on the road. In 2017 the US Department of Transportation will open ten self-driving test tracks across the country for further study. Software engineers are collaborating and combining their efforts today to make self-driving cars a legitimate—and safe—means of transportation in the future.

Jeff Zurschmeide, "How Do Engineers Design Today's Astronomically Complicated Cars? Using These Tools," Digital Trends, October 15, 2016. www.digitaltrends.com.

are out of eggs or low on milk. Cars will text their owners when they need to be serviced. "Case studies show examples where a home monitoring device is able to notice a patient's need to see a doctor, schedule the appointment, call for an Uber ride, and track the patient's health all the way to the doctor's office,"[57] says a software engineer who works for a defense contractor.

According to Dave Evans of the technology company Cisco, the IoT "represents the next evolution of the Internet."[58] He and Cisco's Internet Business Solutions Group estimate that 50 billion objects will be interconnected by 2020. Software engineers will be instrumental in making these products usable, getting them online, and keeping them connected.

Preparing for the Future

One way software engineers can prepare for this dynamic future is by learning other languages. Although expertise in programming languages is beneficial, so too is fluency in spoken languages. "There will be a market for people who speak languages other than English, because companies often interact with teams in foreign countries, and therefore need technologists who understand those cultures and their languages,"[59] says software consultant Chaka Allen.

Future software engineers can also expect to learn about their field in nontraditional ways. For example, Philip Johnson, a professor at the University of Hawaii, likes to think of his students as athletes training for a big game. "In order for my students to feel comfortable participating in a startup weekend or hackathon environment, they need to train for it," he says. "And this means not just learning useful languages, technologies, and design patterns, it also means learning to code *fast*. It means instead of thinking of development in terms of days and weeks, they think in terms of hours and minutes." Johnson views it as his responsibility to train his software engineering students to be agile, flexible, and otherwise fit for the field. "In other words, students need to engage in software development as an *athletic* activity, not a (sedentary) *cubicle* activity."[60]

> "There will be a market for people who speak languages other than English, because companies often interact with teams in foreign countries, and therefore need technologists who understand those cultures and their languages."[59]
>
> —Chaka Allen, independent software consultant

Tomorrow's Problem Solvers

Software engineers will not just be responsible for creating the new digital reality; they will also be charged with solving the problems modern technology may bring. As daily life continues to become infused with computing, technology is becoming more complex. Growth in technology is sure to bring about challenges that software engineers will be asked to solve. "Headlines trumpet software flaws as causing airspace closures, credit card data theft, car and plane malfunctions, unreachable 911 centers, and billions of dollars of wasted taxpayer money," explain the authors of a 2016 IEEE article. "'Smart' objects can use software to cheat and lie, and objects are getting smarter all the time."[61] Still, despite how far software engineers have come, and the progress they have made, they have room to grow and learn.

To be prepared for the future, software engineers need to stay on the cutting edge of their field. Technology changes so fast that relying on the same knowledge or skill is bound to leave an engineer one step behind. Engineers of tomorrow will need to adapt to rapidly changing environments. They will need to continually grow their technical brain by learning new languages, frameworks, and platforms while also maintaining their communication skills by keeping in touch with customers' ever-changing preferences. Ongoing education will be important for keeping the engineer valuable and employable.

As technology infiltrates daily life, careers in software engineering are sure to rise in number and importance. Whether a software engineer works in web application development or cybersecurity; creates phone apps; or maintains antivirus software, payroll and billing systems, or inventories, one thing is sure—the future looks bright.

CHAPTER 7

Interview with a Software Engineer

Jennifer Sirp is a software engineer who worked at Lawrence Livermore National Lab in California for ten years and now owns her own business. She answered questions about her career by e-mail.

Q: Why did you become a software engineer?

A: Honestly? I chose the profession because I wanted to see if I could do it. I didn't know anything about computers when I began in 2000. I was tired of waiting tables . . . and when I was twenty-four I realized that I didn't want to be still working in restaurants when I was thirty. I like challenges and even though I did poorly in high school, I was always smart and tenacious. So, I thought if I was going to go through college (I paid for college myself), I wanted to get a degree that would give me financial freedom. I got a bachelor of science in computer science, and then worked as a Java developer for Lawrence Livermore National Lab for ten years.

Q: Was getting your degree easy, financially or academically?

A: Heck no, I worked my tail off! My parents were unable to help with my college degree financially. I was considered a dependent in the eyes of the state, even though I wasn't living at home or being claimed as a dependent on their taxes. So, I attended a good junior college because it was affordable, and I took everything I could that would transfer. I waited to pursue my degree at Sacramento State University when I was twenty-four so I would be eligible for subsidized loans. Throughout college, I waitressed on the weekends. Academically, I focused on getting excellent grades and only took three or four classes at a time. It took me a little over six years to get my degree. I racked up $30,000 in student loans. But once I graduated, I worked hard to save and was in a position to pay off my loans within two years.

Q: Can you describe your typical workday?

A: A typical workday at the lab was sitting behind my desk in my office writing software, often researching new technologies, frameworks, and toolkits that could be used or integrated with our own in-house tools. Meetings were a couple times a week with all the members of the team and other scientists. Occasionally I gave presentations on what I was working on or about a new technology I had researched.

Q: What did you like most about your job?

A: What I liked most was writing software that was useful to someone: building something that had never existed before to solve a problem or fill a real need. There is a component of software development that is creative, and when you get to design, or start in at the very beginning of a project, it is exciting! There is momentum, collaboration, and excitement that is infectious.

Q: What did you like least about your job?

A: Sitting behind a desk and computer all day! I love the outdoors.

Q: What personal qualities do you find most valuable for this type of work?

A: Determination, organization, problem solving, and the ability to methodically and scientifically approach tasks are most important. It's also important not only to write code that works, but also to be consistent, thorough, and write code that others can understand and test easily. A lot of time, most in fact, is spent debugging your own software or others'. The more straightforward the code is you are working with, the more time and headache it will save you.

Another skill that is less common among computer scientists is communication. A lot of people in this field have poor communication skills; either they struggle with English or are so hard-core into tech that their social skills are lacking. I have found time and time again that if you can speak effectively, and communicate complex ideas and technology, it is easy to advance in the career. You have to be able to explain issues to those more technical and less technical than yourself. If you can do that well, you will be highly valued by your managers.

Q: What surprised you the most about your career as a software engineer?

A: How few women there are in the field! I think the majority of my classes were about 20 percent women. When I started working and after talking to engineer friends, I have found that there are very few female software developers; much fewer than 20 percent of the people I worked with. That may be because the long hours, at least as a developer, are not a friendly environment to work in while raising kids.

Q: What advice do you have for students who might be interested in this career?

A: Computer science and engineering is an excellent career to get into and is very rewarding financially. I advise whoever pursues it to make sure they actually like it in the beginning. Getting the degree is a lot of work, so make sure that you can see yourself doing it for the next ten to twenty years before you fully commit. Another recommendation is to get a job in the industry while you're still in school. It will let you know for sure if you like it, and it will look great on your résumé as you will have relevant work experience. If you think you want to work at Apple or Google, or wherever you are dreaming . . . call someone there who is in a position you are interested in and ask them if you can meet them on site for an "informational interview" where you simply talk about their job, the kinds of things they do on a daily basis, and get a feel for the specific work environment there. Nine times out of ten, people will be happy to do it. Once you are there, you can really see if you like it. Ask lots questions and interview *them*. You want to pick a good match for you just as much as the company wants to find a good match for them.

SOURCE NOTES

Introduction: Technology Is Everywhere
1. Mikko Varpiola, "Software Is Everywhere," Synopsys Software Integrity, August 4, 2015. https://blogs.synopsys.com.
2. Matt Reisner, interview with author, September 12, 2016.

Chapter 1: What Does a Software Engineer Do?
3. Government defense contractor, interview with author, November 12, 2016.
4. Nicholas C. Zakas, "What's a Software Engineer, Anyway?," NCZOnline, June 28, 2012. www.nczonline.net.
5. Matt Reisner, interview with author, January 22, 2017.
6. Bill Draven, interview with author, October 26, 2016.
7. Reisner, interview, January 22, 2017.
8. Ben Kepes, "Cyber Attacks Are on the Rise," Network World, July 19, 2016. www.networkworld.com.
9. Quoted in Kim Martineau, "New Software Continuously Scrambles Code to Foil Cyber Attacks," Data Science Institute, November 17, 2016. http://datascience.columbia.edu.
10. Greg A. Lynch, "Attack on an Industrial Control System Leaves 'Massive Damage' at Steel Plant," ICS Engineering Inc. www.icsenggroup.com.
11. Alex Barinka, "Target's Data Breach: What Went Wrong?," Bloomberg News, June 3, 2014. www.bloomberg.com.
12. Quoted in National Academy of Engineering, "Ask an Engineer," EngineerGirl. www.engineergirl.org.

Chapter 2: How Do You Become a Software Engineer?
13. Quoted in Quora, "How Can I Prepare Myself to Be a Software Engineer at Google?," Software Engineering at Google, September 1, 2014. www.quora.com.
14. Quoted in Maggie O'Neill, "Computer Science Before College," Computer Science Online, 2017. www.computerscienceonline.org.

15. Michael Bolin, "What Are the Most Important Classes for High School Students to Succeed in Software Engineering?," January 18, 2011. http://bolinfest.com.

16. Iliya Koreshev, answer to "What Should I Do Afterschool in High School If I Want to Be a Computer Engineer After College?," CareerVillage, September 30, 2011. www.careervillage.org.

17. Barbara Oakley, "Engineering—the Smart Career Choice for People Who Love Psychology," *Scalliwag* (blog), *Psychology Today*, August 12, 2012. www.psychologytoday.com.

18. Government defense contractor, interview.

19. Chaka Allen, interview with author, October 25, 2016.

20. Draven, interview, October 26, 2016.

21. Mark Russell, interview with author, October 18, 2016.

22. Peter Torelli, interview with author, January 6, 2017.

23. Draven, interview, October 26, 2016.

24. Russell, interview.

Chapter 3: What Skills and Personal Qualities Matter Most—and Why?

25. Quoted in Quora, "How Can I Prepare Myself to Be a Software Engineer at Google?"

26. Quoted in Goodreads, "Yogi Berra: Quotes." www.goodreads.com.

27. Quoted in National Academy of Engineering, "Close Ups," EngineerGirl. www.engineergirl.org.

28. Russell, interview.

29. Draven, interview, October 26, 2016.

30. Russell, interview.

31. Quoted in Masters of Engineering, "15 Qualities Every Software Engineer Should Have," 2017. http://mastersinsoftwareengineering.net.

32. Michael Lant, "Software Development and Creativity," *Michael Lant* (blog), October 25, 2010. http://michaellant.com.

33. Quoted in Quora, "How Can I Prepare Myself to Be a Software Engineer at Google?"

34. Bill Draven, interview with author, November 1, 2016.

35. Quoted in Matt Weisfeld, "What Skills Employers Want in a Software Developer: My Conversations with Companies Who

Hire Programmers," InformIT, November 12, 2013. www
.informit.com.

36. Quoted in Weisfield, "What Skills Employers Want in a Software Developer."

37. Allen, interview, October 25, 2016.

38. Dave Yarwood, "Getting Your First Programming Job Is Not as Hard as You Think," *Tech Blog*, Adzerk, November 17, 2015. https://adzerk.com.

Chapter 4: What Is It Like to Work as a Software Engineer?

39. Chaka Allen, interview with author, November 15, 2016.

40. Owen Pellegrin, "What Does a Software Engineer Do?," *Yeah, It's a Blog*, March 3, 2010. www.owenpellegrin.com.

41. Government defense contractor, interview.

42. Government defense contractor, interview.

43. Quoted in Quora, "How Can I Prepare Myself to Be a Software Engineer at Google?"

44. Quoted in Salvador Rodriquez, "Tech Diversity: Female Software Engineers Earn $10,000 Less than Male Counterparts," *International Business Times*, March 12, 2016. www.ibtimes.com.

45. Jennifer Sirp, interview with author, January 6, 2017.

46. Iliya Koreshev, answer to "What Is the Worst Kind of Day in Your Job in Software Engineering?," CareerVillage, October 3, 2013. www.careervillage.org.

47. Allen, interview, November 15, 2016.

48. Draven, interview, October 26, 2016.

Chapter 5: Advancement and Other Job Opportunities

49. Andy Vargas, interview with author, November 16, 2016.

50. Andriy Buday, "Career Plan for Software Engineer. Do You Have One?" *Developer's Success* (blog), http://andriybuday.com.

51. Allen, interview, October 25, 2016.

52. Chad Fowler, *The Passionate Programmer: Creating a Remarkable Career in Software Development*. Raleigh, NC: Pragmatic Bookshelf, 2009, p. 160.

Chapter 6: What Does the Future Hold for Software Engineers?

53. Alan J. Perlis, "Epigrams on Programming," Core Memory. http://thecorememory.com.
54. Forrest Shull et al., "The Future of Software Engineering," *IEEE Software Magazine*, January/February 2016, p. 33. www.computer.org.
55. Phillip Ball, "Make Your Own World with Programmable Matter," *IEEE Spectrum*, May 27, 2014. http://spectrum.ieee.org.
56. Dries Buytaert, "The Future of Software Is Data-driven," *On Digital Experiences, Open Source, Startups & the Future* (blog), January 8, 2015. http://buytaert.net.
57. Government defense contractor, interview.
58. Dave Evans, "The Internet of Things: How the Next Evolution of the Internet Is Changing Everything," Cisco, April 2011. www.cisco.com.
59. Allen, interview, November 15, 2016.
60. Philip Johnson, "Athletic Software Engineering," Essays, July 12, 2013. http://philipmjohnson.org.
61. Shull et al., "The Future of Software Engineering."

Computer Science Online

www.computerscienceonline.org

Computer Science Online is an in-depth website for students considering a career in computers and software engineering. It offers expert advice and resources to develop important computer science skills, starting from kindergarten through high school. Search tools help students research school programs, articles, guides, and salary data.

Institute of Electrical and Electronics Engineers (IEEE) Computer Society

2001 L St. NW, Suite 700
Washington, DC 20036
www.computer.org

The IEEE Computer Society is the world's leading membership organization dedicated to computer science and technology. With more than sixty thousand members, the volunteer-based, global community of technology leaders includes researchers, educators, software engineers and other IT professionals, employers, and students. It sponsors more than two hundred technical conferences and events each year, including a Rock Stars series aimed at research and industry professionals.

Internships.com

www.internships.com/software

Internships.com is a student-focused internship marketplace. Students can search specifically for software internships and filter by location. Available positions state whether they are part time or full time, paid or voluntary. Most internships are for college students, but some are based on skill sets, not age.

National Science Foundation (NSF)
4201 Wilson Blvd.
Arlington, VA 22230
www.nsf.gov

The NSF is an independent federal agency created by Congress. One of its goals is to promote the progress of science by funding research that allows scientists, engineers, and students to work at the outermost frontiers of knowledge. It also supports science and engineering education, from pre-K through graduate school and beyond, by offering grants and student opportunities for learning.

Society of Women Engineers (SWE)
203 N. La Salle St., Suite 1675
Chicago, IL 60601
http://swe.org

The SWE is a not-for-profit educational and service organization that empowers women to succeed and advance in the field of engineering and to be recognized for their life-changing contributions as engineers and leaders. Created in 1950, the organization looks to expand the image of the engineering profession as a positive force in improving the quality of life and to demonstrate the value of diversity. It offers mentoring and both professional and personal networking.

Technology Student Association (TSA)
1914 Association Dr.
Reston, VA 20191
www.tsaweb.org

The TSA is a national organization of students engaged in science, technology, engineering, and mathematics. It is open to students enrolled in or who have completed technology education courses. Membership includes more than 233,000 middle and high school students—representing approximately two thousand schools in forty-nine states—who learn through competitive events and leadership opportunities.

PICTURE CREDITS

ABOUT THE AUTHOR

You may have seen Bitsy Kemper on CNN, heard her on national radio, or seen her in hundreds of TV shows and newspapers across the country. The author of seventeen books for young readers up to young adults, she has presented in schools, libraries, and conferences all around the United States. She grew up in New York, went to North Carolina for two undergraduate college degrees, and then earned a master of business administration degree in California, where she lives today. Married to an engineer, she and her husband are proudly raising three more potential engineers. When not knee-deep in research or writing whimsical fiction, Kemper is active in church, yoga, and theater.